Cadence, 2016

♡Aunt Mindy

for
TEENAGE GIRLS
with
WILD AMBITIONS
and
TREMBLING
HEARTS

CLEMENTINE VON RADICS

Andrews McMeel
Publishing®
a division of Andrews McMeel Universal

When you are 13 years old,

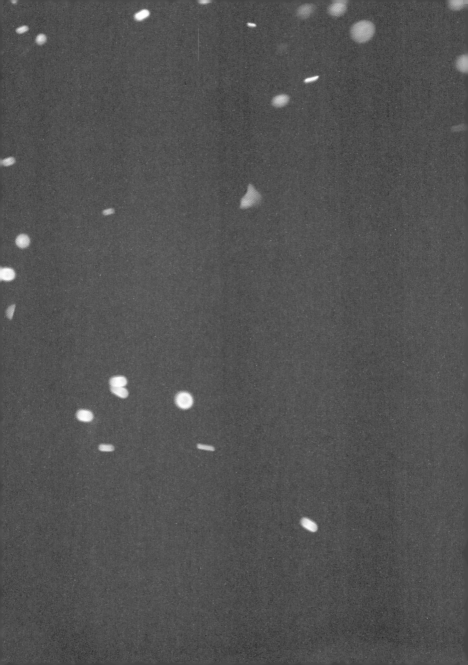

the heat will be turned up too high
and the stars will not be in your favor.

You will hide behind a bookcase
with your family and everything hunted.
You will spend years pouring an ocean
into a diary. When they find you,
they will treat you like nothing more
than a spark above a burning bush.

Still, tell them,
Despite everything,
I really believe people are good at heart.

When you are 14 years old,
a voice will call you to greatness.

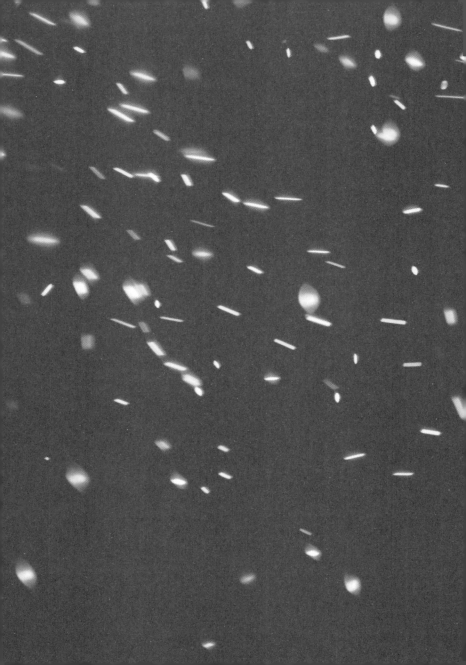

When the doubters call you crazy,
do not listen. They don't know the sound
of their own God's whisper.
Do not let their doubting drown out
the sound of your own heartbeat.

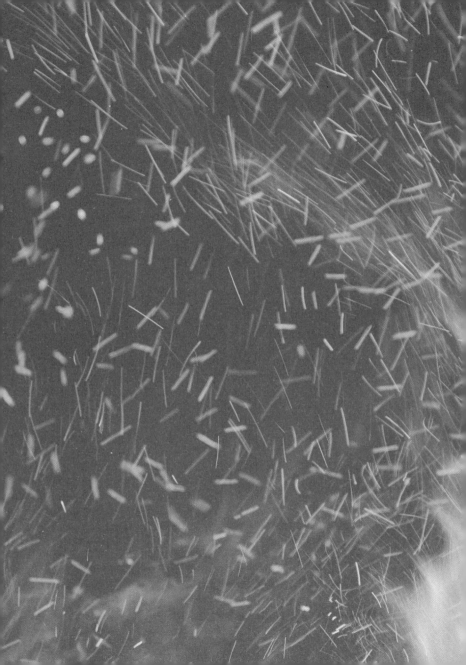

You are the Maid of Untamed Patriotism.
You were born to lead armies
and unite a nation like a broken heart.

When you are 15 years old,
you will be punished
for learning too proudly.

A man will climb onto your school bus
and insist your sisters name you enemy.
When you do not hide, he will point his gun
and fire three times. Three years later,
in an ocean of survival, and no apologies,
you will stand before the leaders
of the world and tell them
how your country is burning.

When you are 16 years old,
you will invent science fiction.
The story of a man named Frankenstein
and his creation. You will soon learn

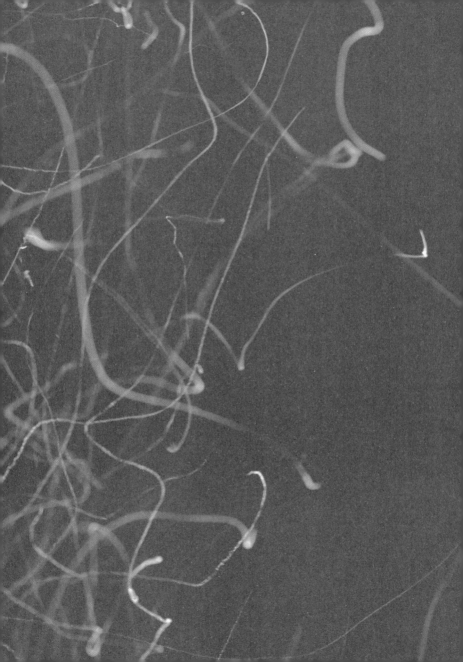

young girls with big ideas
are far more terrifying than monsters.
But don't be afraid. You will be remembered
long after they have put down their torches.

When you are 17 years old,
you will strike out Babe Ruth
then Lou Gehrig, one right after the other.

Grown men will be so afraid of the lightning
in your fingertips that a few days later
all women will be fired
from the major leagues. The reason?
Girls are too delicate to play baseball.

You will turn 18
with a baby on your back,
leading Lewis and Clark
across North America.

You will turn 18
and be queen of the Nile.

You will turn 18
and bring justice to journalism.

You are now 18,
standing on the precipice,

trembling before your own greatness.

This is your call to leap.

There will always be those
who say you are too young and delicate
to make anything happen for yourself.

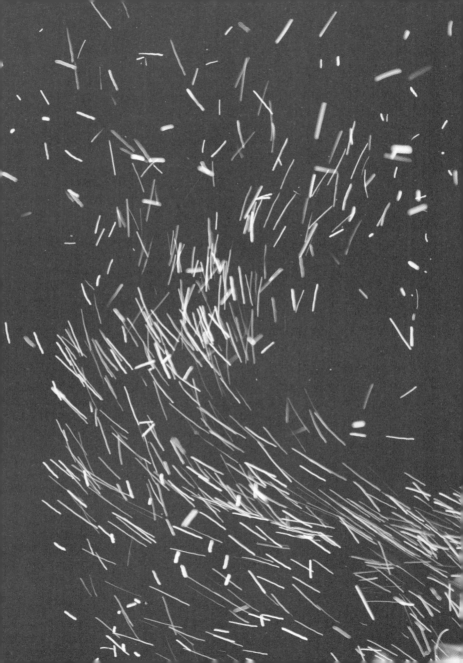

They don't see the part of you that smolders.

Don't let their doubting drown out
the sound of your own heartbeat.

You are the first drop of rain in a hurricane.

Your bravery builds beyond you.

You are needed by all the little girls

still living in secret, writing oceans

made of monsters, and
throwing like lightning.

You don't need to grow up
to find greatness.

You are so much stronger than the world
has ever believed you could be.

The world is waiting for you
to set it on fire. Trust in yourself

and burn.

Clementine von Radics is a poet who lives in
Portland, Oregon. Her previous book with
Andrews McMeel Publishing is *Mouthful of Forevers.*

For Teenage Girls with Wild Ambitions and Trembling Hearts
copyright © 2016 by Clementine von Radics. All rights reserved.
Printed in China. No part of this book may be used or reproduced
in any manner whatsoever without written permission
except in the case of reprints in the context of reviews.

For Teenage Girls with Wild Ambitions and Trembling Hearts was originally
published in *Mouthful of Forevers* as "Advice for Teenage Girls with Wild Ambitions
and Trembling Hearts." Copyright © 2015 by Clementine von Radics.

Andrews McMeel Publishing
a division of Andrews McMeel Universal
1130 Walnut Street, Kansas City, Missouri 64106

www.andrewsmcmeel.com

16 17 18 19 20 SDB 10 9 8 7 6 5 4 3 2 1

ISBN: 978-1-4494-7970-1

Library of Congress Control Number: 2015957755

Editor: Grace Suh
Designer: Julie Barnes
Production Manager: Tamara Haus
Production Editor: Erika Kuster

Attention: Schools and Businesses
Andrews McMeel books are available at quantity discounts
with bulk purchase for educational, business, or sales promotional use.
For information, please e-mail the Andrews McMeel Special Sales Department:
specialsales@amuniversal.com.